The Christmas Riddle

Merry Christmas 11/09

The Answer is Love

The Christmas Riddle

Inspired by a True Story

BY JESS RICHARD ELMQUIST

RISK

Published by Risk Publishing

Text & Illustration Copyright © 2009 by Jess Richard Elmquist
Cover and Book Design by Catherine Rothstein

"The Christmas Carol,"
reprinted from Charles Dickens, *The Christmas Carol*
(New York, The Platt & Peck Co. Copyright, 1905, by The Baker & Taylor Company) Permission of public domain as copyright has expired.

Visit www.thechristmasriddle.com

Printed in the United States of America
First Risk Publishing Edition 2009

Library of Congress Cataloging-in-Publication Data
Elmquist, Jess Richard
The Christmas Riddle/Jess Richard Elmquist

ISBN 978-0-578-04019-6

To:

Miss Pixley, the Giver of the Riddle

Jeremy, the Liver of the Riddle

Joseph and Julia, the Keepers of the Riddle

"I will honor Christmas in my heart, and try to keep it all the year. I will live in the Past, the Present, and the Future. The Spirits of all Three shall strive within me. I will not shut out the lessons that they teach."

- Ebenezer Scrooge, "A Christmas Carol"

Friend ✳ of the Riddle

Giver of the Riddle:

_____

Keeper of the Riddle:

_____

Christmas _____

✳

I believe that miracles and mysteries enter your life

without invitation, but often when you need them

the most. When I was in fourth grade my three year

old brother Jeremy became ill. Not the kind of illness

that kept him in bed for a week unable to go outside

and play. My brother was the kind of ill that put

alarm and worry into the eyes of my parents. He had

been having severe headaches, loosing his balance

and dealing with increasing pain daily. He could

not be consoled and my parents became frantic to

find an answer.

My mom knew there was something desperately wrong long before the doctors did and finally she came to a breaking point. Falling to her knees she asked God to please give her one more year with her baby and then she would let him go. After that the doctors found the brain cancer.

What followed was a whirlwind of multiple surgeries, chemotherapy with radiation, long hospital stays and an unknown future. The illness sent my family into survival mode, spinning out of our normal everyday existence into a life full of miracles and mysteries we are still trying to understand. One of those mysteries came to us through my adventure of the Christmas Riddle.

The journey began when my parents realized that they were having a hard time taking care of my sick brother in the hospital and me at home. This is when my Gramma Rose came for a visit and asked if I wanted to go home with her. I, being young and eager, often speaking before I thought, said yes because my Gramma lived far away and getting there was not possible for a small boy. So it was much to my surprise when the very next day I found myself on my first airplane ride with my Gramma by my side. I remember being scared to leave my family and Jeremy while he was sick, yet I was excited for my own adventure.

Little did I know this would be the beginning of a journey that would change my life forever.

My Gramma and my Granddad Max lived on Mill Street, a beautiful tree-lined neighborhood in Big Rapids, Michigan. My Grandparents lived in a large two and a half story gabled house in the middle of the block. The house was an inviting home, finished all in gray stucco, with a beautiful brick chimney on the side and a broad welcoming porch off the front. Gramma Rose and Granddad Max managed a lively house, full of people coming and going. Two of their six children still lived at home, Uncle Jimmy and Aunt Becky. They were both teenagers that summer and I thought they were the coolest people on earth. My Uncle Jimmy played guitar, had long hair and hip friends who treated me like their team mascot. He taught me many wonderful songs that summer but he will forever be famous in our family history for teaching me the song "500 Miles Away From Home"; when I was indeed five hundred miles away from home. Uncle Jimmy loved me dearly and often tolerated the incessant questions that I asked and the late night, lonely tears that only a displaced 10-year-old roommate could cry. My wonderfully eccentric and busy extended family loved and cared for me, but I often found myself feeling lost in their life and a long way from my home.

Between the homes on Mill Street there was only space enough for a driveway that led to garages in the backyard. Cars had been an afterthought when the neighborhood was built, so the houses were close and the neighbors friendly. Gramma's large front porch was a meeting place with plenty of room to play. On pleasant afternoons I quickly learned how to get a break from the busyness of Gramma's home. On the porch there was a vintage bench swing that hung from the bead board ceiling calling to all who passed to sit and swing awhile. I would often jump on the bench swing all alone and push back and forth with just enough force to graze the railing in the front and keep the swing moving as high as possible.

On one of those busy days I was swinging on the front porch when a pleasant, elderly lady from next door came out to water her plants. She noticed me playing my swing game and smiled saying, "I bet you're Rose's grandson." I was startled and responding quickly, I jumped off the swing and blurted out "Yes, My name is Jess and I'm 10 years old." "Well, well my name is Miss Pixley." She said as she folded her arms and smiled warmly. "I understand you'll be here for a time so you'll need to come over for some tea and cookies." I stood there without saying a word. "You do like tea and cookies don't you young man?" she asked with a laugh in her voice. "Yes, yes I do!" I finally said, "Well, I'm not sure about tea," I responded on second thought, "But I sure do like cookies!" Miss Pixley chuckled at my answer and asked me to come over the next afternoon and I told her that I would. She paused for a moment and looked me in the eyes, as if she needed to really see me. It seemed she was magically looking straight into my heart when she said, "I like you young man, you've got good stuff inside."

The next day was the first of many tea and cookie days with Miss Pixley and our friendship began. I soon discovered that Miss Pixley was wonderful. She stood no more than 5'2", wore only dresses and had a soft face with gray hair always up nicely in a bun. Miss Pixley had lived her whole life in Big Rapids. After teaching elementary school for 35 years she had retired and was now in the business of attending church, tending her garden and growing old. My Gramma told me that as far as she knew Miss Pixley had never married and had lived alone next door for as long as she could remember. She seemed very happy but there was a hint of sadness about her as well. Despite this I immediately loved her company. I think she loved my visits as well because I was happy go lucky, willing to sit and talk, and so full of life.

Her home was a quiet reminder of things past. The parlor was full of antiques and old family pictures. I had never seen a room so full of wonderful things all untouchable but full of mystery and magic. On the days I would visit, Miss Pixley wisely led me to the back of her home to sit and have tea and cookies in a simple kitchen. Often as I walked through the parlor I would try to notice something I hadn't noticed before such as a crystal vase on the windowsill, the framed picture of an old log cabin, or the large steamer trunk in the corner.

Many of my days were spent in the back of her house at the kitchen table. We would talk about the day, eat cookies and tell stories. Miss Pixley had a wonderful sense of humor and being a retired schoolteacher, a great way with children; and I, I had all the time in the world. So there we sat, an odd couple, a spinster lady seeking companionship and a displaced boy trying to find his way in a world away from home.

"I understand that your little brother is sick." said Miss Pixley one afternoon as we sat in the kitchen. The reality of why I was living with my Gramma on Mill Street came to me in a flood. I sat quietly and looked down at my hands as sadness, worry and the scary question of "Why did my brother get sick?" came over me. I had just talked to my Mom and she had said my brother was doing "ok". I had come to understand that when my Mom said "ok" it meant that my

brother Jeremy was not doing very well fighting

his cancer. "You know I have had people close

to me get sick", Miss Pixley said clearly, seeming

not to notice my far off look. "Worry and sadness

are normal Jess," I looked up at her face. She

looked back at me with intense confidence and

wisdom of years. I could see she was sharing

my simple pain of my brother's illness when she

said, "Jess, I'm not sure why Jeremy got sick in

the first place and I'm not sure what is going to

happen with your little brother. What I do know

is that there is hope. Hope is a pathway for you

to take through the pain of life. I have found that

if you can't hold on to hope through pain, you

can't hold on to life. Walk down the path long

enough and the path will lead you back to joy."

She poured a little more tea in both cups, patted

my hand and we said nothing for awhile feeling

the connection grow.

As the weeks of summer passed I found out

that Miss Pixley thought I was funny so I would

try to make her laugh. Often she would throw

up her hands and look up into the sky and

say, "Mercy me if you aren't full of silly stuff."

and then she'd laugh again. Miss Pixley found

out I loved Christmas time most of all and she

would tell me wonderful stories of Christmas

memories from when she was a little girl. She

would tell tales of cold nights on the Pixley farm

sledding in the snow and horse drawn sleigh

rides. With a twinkle in her eyes she talked about her Daddy, their family time around the dinner table, homemade gifts under the tree, the smell of cookies baking, the taste of her mother's pumpkin pie, reading by candlelight, and the mystery of the Christmas Riddle.

"What is the Christmas Riddle?" I asked. "Oh, it's not a what, but a whom," replied Miss Pixley with a gleam in her eye. I was curious. I would ask her from time to time what the Christmas Riddle was all about and each time she would say, with a distant look in her eye, "Oh there is power in the Riddle, the answer young man will have to wait for the snow to fall."

As early spring turned into summer and then summer faded to autumn, word came that Jeremy was recovering and coming home from the hospital. The time had come for me to go back to Minnesota, back to my sick brother, back to a new school year and back to all the uncertainty that was sure to come with this change. I had reached the end of my adventure and was surprised to find the place that had felt so strange only months before had become like home. I was now torn, having to face my real life with all the unknowns and leave this warm, familiar place I had come to trust. I was suddenly scared to go back home.

The day came when I had to leave Gramma Rose, Mill Street and the family I had come to know so well. On the day I had to say goodbye to Miss Pixley, I slowly wandered over to her home for tea and cookies. She invited me in and was strangely quiet compared to the other days we had spent together. She knew that it was time for me to leave and the companionship that I had given would be gone. The hours spent in the kitchen that summer had in one way released the energy of life in her again and now those times were coming to an end.

As I took the normal path through the parlor to the kitchen, Miss Pixley stopped me short and led me to the parlor couch, "We'll have our last treats in here today," she said. I was amazed! The magical parlor room came alive with soft light shining through an ancient Tiffany lamp. The familiar tea and cookies were on a table waiting for us. We sat and chatted about home and the fun time we had together over the summer.

Before I left my Gramma's house she had reminded me to say thank you for all the time I had spent with Miss Pixley. That reminder was not needed as I felt overwhelmed by her kindness and care. As a ten-year-old I was at a loss for the right words. I welled up with emotion as the time came to leave and with tears coming to my eyes I looked up to see tears in her eyes as well. For the first time that summer she patted my hand and wouldn't let go. "I have something for you", she said while she got up and led me to the corner of the parlor. She stopped us in front of the large steamer trunk I had noticed before. It was a striking midnight blue and lined with brass latches and leather trim. The brass corners were worn with years of use and there were traditional symbols of Christmas painted on every side; Christmas trees, a horse and sleigh and wrapped presents lined the base. On the top of the trunk was a painted picture of Father Christmas and his reindeer. They were soaring over a sleepy little town with the full moon casting a glow of light over his shoulder. The picture seemed to take life, as if Father Christmas were racing on his way with a "HO, HO, HO Merry Christmas!"

into the frozen night. What a wonderful trunk!

"This trunk hasn't been opened for a very long time," she said, her voice fading as the hinges creaked and the contents became visible. "Here are all the Christmas decorations from when I was a little girl. My family loved Christmas like you do. These are all of our greatest Christmas treasures." I could not believe my eyes. There were gold, red, green and blue ornaments of every shape and size with finely painted winter scenes on the glass. A beautiful angel, awaiting the top of a tree, sat partially wrapped in a satin bag. Painted wood candy canes were lined neatly in their boxes and gingerbread men all held hands as if they were dancing in a line. There

was a photo album, an ancient snow globe, toy soldiers, a Nutcracker and right on top, sitting on an old family bible, was a box that read, "The Christmas Riddle."

Miss Pixley waited for my eyes to catch the words and then she said, "I want you to have the Christmas Riddle. My Daddy made the Christmas Riddle box for our family a long time ago. Please take it as a gift, but you have to promise not to open it until Christmas Day, after the snow begins to fall." I looked up at Miss Pixley, but she was no longer in the room. The trunk and its treasure had transported her to a far away time and place. She had a slight smile of nostalgia and tears were filling her eyes. I waited to speak, watching the memories run across Miss Pixley's face. Finally she came back to me and as I picked up the Christmas Riddle Box I promised not to open the box until the snow began to fall. The box was red and green and painted in detail with golden stars and symbols of the Christmas holiday. On the top it read, "CR, The Christmas Riddle" and all around the outside was the riddle written in gold. The riddle read, "What gift is small, yet larger than all?" I stood there puzzled until Miss Pixley put her hand on my shoulder and slowly closed the trunk. She lingered there a moment fingering the brass lock as if she were still living a life from the past that the trunk brought back to her. I wondered what she was thinking and why the memories seemed to make her as sad as they did happy. With a breaking voice I thanked her again for the amazing gift. She looked at me and said, "Oh, Christmas is such a joy filled time, but when you get as old as I am, some pain gets mixed in too. You'll find Jess that Christmas is big enough to hold both because Christmas holds life. You wait until Christmas to open the box just as I always had to do. My Daddy always said that the fun was in the waiting." I shook my head in agreement and assured her that I would wait. We said goodbye and putting the new gift down I embraced this graceful woman with all the appreciation within my heart. As Gramma Rose walked slowly across the yard to gather me home I said "I love you Miss Pixley!."

"I love you too boy." she said, "Use all that good stuff inside to find your path to joy."

Before we parted Gramma had us stand together for a picture. "Now go back home but don't you forget Miss Pixley when you are gone." she said. Wiping my eyes I looked at her for the last time as I picked up the gift and walked toward Gramma's house holding precious Miss Pixley in my heart and the special gift tightly with both hands.

When I finally arrived home I found that it had not changed as much as I had that summer. The house was just the same and my younger brother was still recuperating from the cancer. My Mom and Dad were happy to see me. My Mom wanted to know all about my time away so I told her the story of Miss Pixley, the magical parlor, tea and cookies and of course the Christmas Riddle. My Mother just listened and then said with a knowing look, "I know Miss Pixley, I grew up right next door to her. I also know about "The Christmas Riddle". My mom got up, kissed the top of my head and gently picking up the gift from where it sat she said, "We'll just pack this box away and wait for Christmas Day after the snow begins to fall". "The snow to fall?", my mother did know the riddle! The mystery grew as I longed to know the secret held inside the box. She packed away the gift with a smile, excited for my anticipated discovery.

The fall wore on. School started and I wondered if Christmas would ever come so I could discover the answer to the riddle, "What gift is small, yet larger than all?" The riddle would dance in my mind day after day. Then one day, the snow finally began to fall and Christmas was within sight. As we did every year my family went to the country and cut down a tree. My mom set up the Advent candles to welcome in the season. We began to prepare for Christmas with the usual traditions of baking Hungry Boy cookies, holiday parties, listening to Christmas music, shopping for those special gifts and the wrapping of presents. The Christmas Riddle box came out and rested under the newly decorated tree. There it sat, daily joined by a growing pile

of other gifts, although none were as intriguing as the Christmas Riddle.

My brother and I shared a room and on Christmas morning Jeremy woke up first. I felt him tapping my shoulder and saying, "Brover, brover, its time to open prethenst." Rubbing my eyes, I rolled over and saw him smiling with excitement ready to open gifts! In a moment I recognized that this was going to be a good day for Jeremy. He had the energy of a healthy little boy. Besides his bald little head from radiation he was acting like a normal three year old. That was exciting to me and I knew that my parents would see his energy that morning as the ultimate gift.

We crept out of our room to find the house alive with the lights, sounds and smells of our favorite day. Dad had been up early preparing the Christmas meal while mom wrapped one last package. My brother and I raced to the tree and were greeted with the glitter of the lights. Typically, we could be found shaking gifts and guessing what was inside, but not this time. My parents came out with coffee in hand to find their children waiting with only one gift between them. We were poised and ready to open the gift from Miss Pixley. We gathered round the tree and I picked up the box and read the words out loud, "What gift is small, yet larger than all?" With great anticipation I opened the top of the first box to reveal the contents inside.

Inside the first box top was written, "The gift is the answer and the answer is the gift." More riddles, I just couldn't wait! I looked at my brother and his eyes were glued to the boxes while my Mother looked on with a smile. My mind went to Miss Pixley and how many times she must have touched this same box as a little girl. I wondered what she was doing right then on Christmas morning, so far away, and I missed her. I looked into the box only to see another box! Miss Pixley had quite a sense of humor. There were more boxes inside, and I was amused, thinking that wherever she was she might be laughing. On the second box was a word I had read before...

✴

HOPE

Under the word it said, "Hope is that feeling that something special is coming." Behind the word hope was a gleaming star painted with iridescent color and the star came alive as it caught the light of the tree. Anxious to solve the riddle I opened the next lid and looked in only to find another box! I carefully lifted it out. This box was more finely finished than the first or the second. This one had a word large and strong written on the top. Around the word it read, "Peace knows that what you hope for is finally here."

✳

PEACE

I realized by this time that the Christmas Riddle was not an ordinary gift, the kind of gift that you tore the paper off of just so you could get to the next present. However, I was getting strangely excited as the boxes grew smaller. The gift made me think. Although I wanted to know what came next I slowed down and studied the pictures and symbols around each side of the box. I was captured in the moment. A voice in my head and heart said, "Wait, look, see, and learn about this gift." I opened the third box only to find yet a fourth box with a word on the top that brought Miss Pixley to mind, the cookies and tea and the subtle lessons taught during our summer together.

✳

JOY

Around the word joy in small gold letters it read, "The small gift brings JOY!" The box was brightly decorated with colors that danced in my eyes, never had a box at Christmas been a gift all by itself. We all stared at the box and were in some way content to stay here and not open any others. To stay at joy, a precious gift all on its own. Joy was the feeling we had as we celebrated Christmas with each other that morning. I looked up at my Mom and Dad. They were holding each other's hand, looking down at my younger brother peering at the gifts. In my parent's eyes was the pain and sadness of their son's illness, but way down beyond sadness was hope leading to joy that no amount of pain could take away. My Mom and Dad really did know the answer to the Christmas Riddle.

In those first moments on that Christmas morning, I had gone from a boy in desperate need to know the answer to the riddle; to a boy that was willing to look at the boxes and ponder the clues. I was willing to let the gift uncover its own mysterious answer as the boxes got smaller.

The box entitled; "Joy" was quite small. I somehow knew that there were not many boxes left until I uncovered the answer: yet suddenly, looking at Jeremy healing from cancer, my heart wrenched. His bald head, chemo and radiation ravaged body was still here! My brother was still here! Right then my childhood Christmas

changed as hot tears of sadness and joy came

into my eyes and Miss Pixley's voice came back

to me, "Oh Christmas is such a joy filled time,

but when you get as old as I am, some pain gets

mixed in too. You'll find Jess that Christmas

is big enough to hold both because Christmas

holds life."

My shoulders heaved with a sob. My Mom and

Dad looked at me with concern yet waited and

watched. I leaned up on my knees, hugged my

brother and gave him the gift of joy. He deserved

the opportunity to open "Joy." He was alive and

getting healthier every day. Yes, joy was what he

needed. He opened the box and inside he pulled

out an even smaller box with a familiar word on top. My brother looked up and said, "Brover, it says Lo-lov-love." The smallest box entitled LOVE had two symbols in the background that I recognized. Painted in a dusting of gold was a manger where the Christ child was born and then a painted cross intersected the manger and rose from behind.

Then it hit me. "What gift is small, yet larger than all?" Not just hope, peace and joy but those symbols brought the largest gift of all, love. Love brought the Christ child to earth and love brought Christ the man to the cross.

✳

LOVE

My brother opened the box marked "LOVE" and within the box, wrapped in satin, sat a beautiful glass star shaped ornament. He picked up the star from the box. On the star was the same symbol. On one side was the manger and on the other side a cross. The cross intersected the manger through the star. My brother handed me the star and I read the line written above the manger, "What gift is small..." and then turned it over to read under the cross, "yet larger than all?"

As we passed the precious ornament around that morning the same warmth came to our eyes and delicacy to our touch. Perhaps we all felt the power of those who had discovered the riddle before us and we wanted to linger in their company. With all the other brightly wrapped packages still untouched under the tree, we were content to hold HOPE, PEACE, JOY and LOVE.

I got it! The Christmas Riddle was discovered as I opened the gift. In opening the boxes I found out that the gift is the answer and the answer is the gift. The riddle was right! I hung the ornament in the center of our tree that morning while my father read the Christmas story. Once again Miss Pixley changed me. She had passed a wonderful gift to our family that year. In one way, she wanted to show a young boy the truth about Christmas. Also, she had never had children and needed a family to pass on her special tradition. She found a boy who loved

Christmas and she knew the Christmas Riddle

would live on for years to come.

$$\times$$

In the summers that followed, my family often

made the long journey to Michigan to visit

Gramma Rose and Granddad Max. During

those visits I could be found in the back of Miss

Pixley's house, eating cookies and drinking tea.

As I grew I came to a greater appreciation of

the relationship I had with Miss Pixley and in

some ways I believe I became the son she always

wanted. Many times during the year we would

communicate by letter or phone just to say

hello. Every Christmas Miss Pixley would get

a card that told her who my family had shared the Christmas Riddle with that year. The gift's magic never faded. The power of the message became more real as my family grew.

I was in my last year of college, just before holiday break, when I received a call from Gramma Rose. Miss Pixley was in the hospital. She had recently fallen, broken her hip and she was not doing well. The prognosis was grave and just that evening she had asked about me. Within an hour of the call I was in my car and making the long drive to Big Rapids. As I drove those long miles I knew that my journey would bring me to a destination I did not want to face; yet I hoped that I would get there in time to help her like she had helped me so many years before.

When I finally arrived, Gramma Rose and I immediately went to the hospital and found Miss Pixley's darkened room. The streetlight from her window was casting a golden glow across her bed and there she was, the wonderful Miss Pixley. So fiercely independent for so long she now looked completely helpless in the large hospital bed. I took her hand and gently kissed her on the forehead. Her eyes opened and as they focused I said with a whisper, "Hello, Miss Pixley." "Boy!" she said weakly realizing it was me, "You didn't forget about me, you came to say good bye." A sadness came over me as I said, "Yes, I've come to say good bye."

Miss Pixley closed her eyes as she moved her small body in order to find a more comfortable position, tears flowed down her face as she whispered to me, "I just want to go home". I wiped the tears from her eyes, I looked back at my Gramma, confused, not knowing what to do. Gramma leaned down and spoke gently into my ear. "Have patience Jess, there's nothing you can fix. Miss Pixley's life is slowing down. She is in God's hands and His home is welcoming her. Remind her of what she has meant to you, her time is growing short." At that my Gramma left to find a nurse and I sat down at her bedside. With determination she focused her gaze on me and we began to talk like we did in that little kitchen on Mill Street. We discussed school; she always wanted to know about my school. She asked how Jeremy was doing and we reminisced about our times together, the letters we had written through the years, the first summer we met and the Christmas' we cherished. Finally Miss Pixley paused and looked in my eyes with a look only she could give. In that moment I said, "Thank you Miss Pixley, for your love, your care and for the story of the Christmas Riddle. You have changed my life and I will always remember you."

"You're a good boy. I always said you were full of good stuff." she reached up briefly to touch my face. Her hand lowered and her face faded into a peaceful smile. As we finished our talk

Miss Pixley's eyes went over my shoulder and focused far off. "I sure have loved this life but I miss the farm and time with my Daddy. I think I'll spend this Christmas at home with him, he's been waiting for me and I'm ready." she said as a familiar twinkle left her tired face. I gently squeezed her hand, she closed her eyes and I seemed to hear her say, "Hi Daddy." Her breath left and she was gone. She had stepped through to home.

I was caught once again saying good-bye before I had planned, to this wonderful woman who had changed my life. I knew that she was home. But I also began to understand that as I grew my memories of life and my memories of Christmas were becoming more like hers. They contained both a mix of joy and pain. The pain of my brother's past illness and the battles he had fought in order to survive weighed heavy on my heart and now, with the loss of Miss Pixley it seemed too much to bear. Yet in that instant, I understood a mystery through a life well lived and the miracle of the Christmas Riddle. Hope is the path through pain that leads back to joy. Miss Pixley was once again teaching and giving me a gift. Slowly I sat up and wiped my eyes as my Gramma Rose returned to the room with a nurse. Gramma Rose hugged my shoulders tightly as I looked out the window and realized that the snow had begun to fall.

The Christmas Riddle Song

Lyrics by Jess Richard Elmquist

A mother holds her sick son
On a silent, snowy night
The Christmas lights are gleaming,
Glowing soft and bright
She is waiting for a miracle,
She is praying for it to come
A riddle growing in her heart,
Why my young one?

Her boy, he's finally sleeping,
His pain is gone for now.
She sits before the Christmas tree,
Tired, head bowed
Tears are running down her face,
Wondering what more that she could do
Just then a voice calls out, it's not about you

Remember Christmas is for hoping
Christmas time's for peace
Christmas time's to pray for joy
That it will soon increase
Yet when the pain invades the season
We're invited to understand
That the answer to this riddle is love.

Her questions still they echoed,
And the riddle it's growing strong
How could a season made for Joy
Make her son wait this long?
She could not come to say it,

Yet it's right there within her heart
If love is the reason, how does pain play a part?

Finally exhausted, asleep but still aware
Wanting to believe, but burdened by her fear
In her weakness came a voice of love,
And it spoke into her heart
It began with a whisper and then she took part

Remember Christmas is for hoping
Christmas time's for peace
Christmas time's to pray for joy
That it will soon increase
Yet when pain invades the season
We're invited to understand
That the answer to the riddle is love.

Now awake she sees the angel,
Looking down from 'top the tree.
She went to her son's bedside,
Got down upon her knees
She touched his tender little face
And prayed with all her might
That the joy of this season
Would fill her son tonight

The boy, he stirred so gently,
His face now showing peace
In this miracle moment,
Her question now released
The promises of Christmas,
A gift from the One above
She joined the choir of angels,
In this chorus of love

Remember Christmas is for hoping
Christmas time's for peace
Christmas time's to pray for joy
That it will soon increase
Yet when pain invades the season
We're invited to understand
That the answer to the riddle is love.

Right then she put her faith back
Into the Master's hands
Just like the Christmas story
The pain's part of God's plan

Remember Christmas is for hoping
Christmas time's for peace
Christmas time's to pray for joy
That it will soon increase
Yet when pain invades the season
We're invited to understand
That the answer to the riddle is love

Yet when pain invades the season
We're invited to understand
That the Christmas Riddle's answer...
The answer is love.

The Christmas Riddle

Acknowledgements

Thank you to Paula Vento who not only edited the story, she felt the story and that made such a difference.

The book was designed by the incredibly talented Catherine Rothstein who listened to what I imagined and made it better.

To Risk Publishing for taking the risk so the reader wouldn't have to.

To Scottie Bahr, Pete and Kim Brunner who together brought "The Christmas Riddle Song" alive with their talent both musically and in the studio. Your work has blessed many.

To my friend, partner and wife Jennifer, who holds me in the riddle of her love. Thank you for believing and working right along with me.

www.thechristmasriddle.com